Insider's Guide to Forex Trading

Discover All of the Insider Techniques That the Pros Are Using With Great Success

Contents

Chapter 1: What the Stock Market Is All About

Chapter 2: Stock Market Trends

Chapter 3: An Introduction to Forex

Chapter 4: Understanding Currency Conversion

Chapter 5: Understanding Statistics

Chapter 6: Forex Volatility and Market Expectation

Chapter 7: Aspects Of The Trade

Chapter 8: Risk Management

Chapter 9: "Buzz" Words

Chapter 10: Expert Trading Options

Chapter 11: Other Trading Options

Chapter 12: In Review

Chapter 13: One Final Option

Chapter 1: What the securities market is All About

In any business or moneymaking venture, preparation and foreknowledge are the keys to success. Without this kind of insight, the try to make a profitable financial decision can only end in disaster and failure, irrespective of your level of motivation and determination or the number of cash you propose to take a position.

In the stock exchange, this rule applies to the nth degree, as you're investing your own money in what may well be considered a high risk wager, and you're wiggling with fire if you are doing not have a minimum of a general background of how it functions. Since having a background in any area is useful in guiding you down a path in this particular region, the more solid your basis of investment knowledge is, the more likely you're to cash in on any try to trade on the open market.

In some ways, trading on the stock exchange are often compared to driving – you are doing not must be an expert to induce behind the wheel of a car, though you're expected to possess some previous knowledge about basic traffic laws, including moving violations, safety regulations, and other legal vehicular infractions, which are learned through either specific study and coursework or perhaps through some type of simple exposure (such because the years you've got spent riding along with your parents et al. who have driven for years). you must be ready to comprehend the essential tools wont to navigate a car (where the break pedal is found versus the gas, and the way to use the car mirror, for example), whether or not you've got never touched a hand wheel.

The same is true in entering the globe of the exchange. While you are doing not should know all the terminology (you won't be short sale or determining your own long and short positions initially, so you are doing not should understand these references completely, though you must bear in mind of them), you ought to certainly be versed within the basic functionality of trading stocks, bonds, securities, and other commodities. And a bit like someone who is behind the wheel of a car and preparing to the touch the throttle for the primary time, you ought to start out with caution and work your way in slowly. a primary time driver will first set the mirrors to his or her own liking, then put the car geared, search for any interfering traffic, and ease onto the throttle, never flooring it and testing the engine initiating of the gate on the primary attempt. Likewise, once you select your first investment, you ought to choose something stable with little fluctuation and not invest an outsized sum of cash on this first venture.

When an individual is learning to drive, he or she is going to be among another individual who is tried and true and might assist them in making better driving decisions and offering corrections that may aid in learning to handle the car more efficiently. within the exchange, there are stockbrokers and other experts who can offer you input and advice to assist you in building your knowledge of the commodities within which you're interested, essentially "steering" you toward better exchange buying and selling decisions.

You could spend hours and hours researching the securities market and its functionality, learning the way to get entangled within the trade and who to contact to urge within the game, especially if your interest lies within the exchange Market, which works far beyond the extent of complication of the domestic stock exchange. However, during this book, you may find all the essential information you wish to urge started down the trail to trading success. All of the leg work and hard research has been in dire straits you, collecting the information and knowledge into one source from which you'll be able to gain enough insight to create you a successful trader on the open market. All you have got to try to to is read so as to realize knowledge and wisdom, step by step that may bring you to a heady level of success. during this ebook, you'll find all such helpful information, all brought together in one single source for simple reference.

How Investment Works

Any time you're visiting be putting your money into a fund; it's a decent idea to start out by understanding what you're buying into. The securities market may be a complicated entity, and doing minimal business in trading requires a good amount of basic knowledge, further because the understanding and acceptance of the high risk factor. The more you recognize before regarding the functionality of the system, the less likely it's that you simply will take a significant hit, ending in devastating loss.

First of all and doubtless most vital within the trading business, you ought to understand what stocks actually are. after you buy or sell a stock on the open market, you ought to detain mind that you just are handling real objects, not pieces of paper; you're buying and selling real parts of a selected company, its product, or another various commodity.

Owning a "share" means you've got actually bought into the corporate or product involved and become a partial owner of that commodity. Of course, you'll be one in all countless shareholders, as most companies and products are broken into minute pieces of the entire, but you're still considered an investor in this company or product until you sell your shares.

Think of it as paying for a tank of gas within the car that your parents bought for you to drive. you'll have even bought the filter that has been placed on the car, and you'll feel that this investment causes you to part owner. However, after you observe the general cost of the car, you've got really contributed little to it amount. However, as long as you still invest within the gas for the car and be sure of the upkeep needs, you'll claim part ownership of the car.

Because the worth of an organization and its products or services can fluctuate continuously, the worth of the stocks you hold won't be the identical from day to day and might sometimes even change hourly. When the worth per share drops and is taken into account low, it's a perfect time to get. this is often the smallest amount expensive thanks to begin your trading venture, and dealing with a stock broker will allow you to achieve more information on what stocks are ripe for the acquisition at any given time.

In doing so, you become a stockholder, and therefore the value of your holdings will fluctuate from day to day. Your gamble (and hope!) is that the worth of the corporate or product during which you've got invested will increase or rebound from the low price at which you made your purchase. this can be the goal of all traders and means your stock will become more valuable.

As the value of your securities increases, so does your net worth. When the worth of the stock in your possession reaches a division, it's time to sell, making a profit on your original investment. Ideally, you'll always sell your holdings for a fairly higher price than the acquisition amount and may never sell when this value of the stock is below your initial terms. it's important to create sure that you simply don't purposely take a net loss because there are lots of occasions once you may be forced to require a loss.

For example, if you buy shares of a corporation at twenty dollars each, you ought to never sell them for eighteen dollars apiece. If possible, you wish to carry off until they're each worth perhaps forty dollars, in essence doubling your money. Of course, this is often just an example, and not all stocks will ever double in value, but the illustration is meaningful.

There are other, more complex ways to take a position within the securities market. However, very similar to learning to ride a bicycle, you are doing not want to form your first attempt without training wheels.

Making Decisions within the Beginning

Let us return to driving as a reference. After you first start driving, you'll not enter the highway and take the car at speeds of sixty and seventy miles per hour. Instead, you'll stay in residential areas or a minimum of on the road, where there's less pressure to keep up such a high speed. within the securities market, you'll also want to remain far away from any expensive stocks or extremely volatile investments until you've got become extremely comfortable with the method of trading.

There are small investment opportunities cited as "penny stocks", which can facilitate your undertake your sea legs and acquire a condole with how the securities market works before investing large sums of cash and risking an enormous loss. These particular stocks cost literally pennies or small dollar amounts and typically only fluctuate fractions of a cent on any given day, making them extremely safe for those just starting out.

Once you get the hang of it and might better judge the market trends, you'll be able to comfortably locomote to more complicated and adventurous areas of the market. it's like removing the training wheels from your bicycle or entering the freeway the primary time at an hour of the day when there's no traffic to wear down.

Be aware that, similar to you'll fall off your bike once or twice and find yourself with some scrapes and bruises, you will lose money in an investment here and there. this can be very typical, and investing within the exchange could be a lot like gambling. In poker, you cannot expect to win every hand, and therefore the same is true within the world of investments. Learning to observe the market trends, though, is comparable to watching other cars as you join traffic and determining the proper speed and proximity to other cars for optimal safety. Such diligent study can facilitate your improve your statistics drastically in a very short time.

Chapter 2: exchange Trends

Understanding securities market trends can make your job of earning money within the market much simpler. In contrast, if you recognize little or nothing about these trends can cause serious loss.

Bulls and Bears

As you dig deeper into the market and learn more about the way it functions, you'll begin to listen to certain terms about marketing trends that appear to be repeated over and once again. Market trends are variable and volatile, both on a routine and over extended periods of your time. Within the past, for instance, the U.S. has had devastating securities market crashes, but because of the liberty of a capitalist society, the American economy has always eventually rebound.

What does it mean for the market or a specific stock to rebound? Assuming that the worth of an organization or its stock has plummeted to A level that appear unrecoverable, leaving it practically worthless, it's going to feel like that company is in peril of bankruptcy and deterioration the scope of the trade markets altogether. All of a sudden, however, the founding father of that company may introduce a brand new product over which consumers go wild. Everyone wants one, and this product could also be briefly supply upon its introduction, causing a race to the retail store shelves.

When such a move occurs, the law of supply and demand will take over, making the corporate valuable yet again. The stock price for that company's shares will recover, and therefore the resulting gain in value would be considered a rebound – a return to the first status (or better) before the devastating loss.

The market trends either up or down, and there are specific references to strong changes within the market values that you just may frequently hear. If several different areas of the market are during a steep downward slide, with values dropping rapidly (perhaps even ten or simple fraction in an exceedingly few days), it's observed as a securities industry. you'll be able to remember this reference like you're within the extremely dangerous position of being chased by a bear – if you're in possession of several stocks or other commodities worth a goodly sum, you've got a heavy chance of losing a good deal of import that might translate to a loss of net worth must you prefer to sell, and it is the same, very dangerous situation.

Your best bet in these cases is to either sell before prices drop below your original terms or to carry onto the shares until the market rebounds. However, when the securities industry reaches an occasional point, it is a perfect time to induce into the sport, because it is rare for prices to drop below this time. Then, if you patiently await the recovery or rebound of the market, you'll be able to make a good deal of cash from a market. These options are discussed in additional depth in later chapters.

At the identical time, a securities industry may be a strong general upward trend for several stocks. You may compare this to the running of the bulls in Pamplona, Spain, every year. You're safer if you're indoors when the running occurs, and by the identical token, if you own stock during a securities industry, you're during a prime position to extend your net worth and sell your shares, making an excellent deal of cash. This is often another idea are further explored in greater detail further on during this e-book.

The Market Outlook

By being attentive of varied changes within the status of various available stock options, you may learn the way to identify early market trends, providing you with a clue to the longer term of a selected commodity, and this may only augment your chances for profitability. Prediction could be a big a part of the sport when working within the stock exchange, since you'll never be completely certain in what direction the market will swing at any given time.

However, you'll be able to make an informed guess, much the identical way a meteorologist forecasts the weather. While he or she isn't right 100% of the time, the forecast is sometimes quite near the particular outcome of the weather because the meteorologist could be a scientist who has studied weather trends and may select details that assist in making that educated guess. With a bit time and seasoning, you'll attain the identical level of experience and intuition within the stock exchange.

Once you've got become easier functioning within the same world because the stockbrokers and day traders, and you are feeling confident (or a minimum of less nervous or awkward) making such important financial decisions, you will plan to make your move toward the interchange Market (more commonly referred to as Forex), and therefore the goal of this book is to organize you to control within the boundaries of this more complex entity. Next, we are going to discuss a number of the properties of Forex and the way more complex this exchange entity is than a typical domestic market.

The exchange Market is incredibly volatile, and there are lots more factors to contemplate when placing an order on this market than on a domestic market. The subsequent chapter is an introduction to the exciting and somewhat scary world of the interchange Market, or Forex.

Chapter 3: An Introduction to Forex

Forex is that the nickname for the interchange Market. Within the U.S, there are several branches of the stock exchange, each with their own name. For example, some stocks trade on the stock market index, others on Nasdaq. Of course, all exchange transactions within the u.s happen on the big apple stock market (NYSE). In other countries the identical is true. There could also be one or more distinct markets.

However, international trade takes place on the market termed the exchange Market, or Forex. Several countries across the globe in almost each time zone participate in trade on Forex, with multiple currencies being utilized and stocks and commodities from all participating countries being offered for trade. Because there are such a big amount of nations and time zones involved, Forex doesn't function as a "business day" entity like most domestic stock markets. It remains open for trade 24 hours every day, 5 days every week.

Of course, these additional hours increase the chance factor intensely for those folks who are human and clearly cannot monitor our investments 24 hours on a daily basis. This suggests that the worth of your holdings could potentially plummet overnight, while you sleep, because other countries are still trading while you're during a dream world. Again, it's sort of a car – there are many moving pieces under the hood, and simply because you can not see them doesn't mean they're not functioning.

This is one reason for several safety options, like limit orders, which we'll discuss later. this can be also why it's strongly recommended that your first attempts to create money on the exchange don't seem to be transactions that happen within the exchange Market but on a regular nine-to-five domestic trading market. In our car analogy, this might be admire having asked someone who has never driven or perhaps changed the oil during a car to rebuild the engine.

Forex Functionality

While the functionality of Forex is that the same as a domestic securities market, the commodities and costs are more volatile, and there are additional factors to require into considerations besides the standard risks related to a domestic market. you may should cope with not only the worth of your stocks and your currency, but also the foreign currencies involved in any trades or exchanges on

Forex, further because the inconsistencies of values of particular goods and services across international borders. it's like driving a car with a customary transmission as opposition an automatic. On the domestic front, the work is generally in deep trouble you, and every one you've got to try and do is navigate, very similar to a transmission. However, shifting gears is kind of just like having to constantly participate within the currency conversion. It may be distracting, and it certainly complicates the act of driving.

Because the financial situation of the many countries isn't as secure as that of the u. s., this may pose a formidable problem in determining where to take a position your money and what to expect next within the international market. Knowing what countries and currencies are involved in Forex can assist you by allowing you to more closely monitor the financial situation within the nations with which you'll be interacting.

The History of Forex

When foreign trade began, it had been not a global trade market. It absolutely was borne out of the Bretton Woods agreement in 1944, which set forth that foreign currencies would be fixed against the dollar, which was valued at $35 per ounce of gold. This precedent was first put into practice in 1967, when a bank in Chicago refused to fund a loan to a professor in sterling pound. Of course, his intention was to sell the currency, which he felt was priced too high against the dollar, then decease back later when the worth had declined, turning a fast profit.

After 1971, when the dollar was now not convertible to gold and therefore the domestic market was stronger, the Bretton Woods agreement was abandoned, and also the currency conversion process became more variable. This allowed for a stronger backing within the foreign markets, and also the U.S. and Europe began a powerful trade relationship. Within the 1980s, the market hours and usage was extended through the utilization of computers and technology to incorporate the Asian time zones further. At this point, exchange equaled about $70 billion every day. Today, about twenty years later, the trade level has skyrocketed, with trade equaling near $1.5 trillion daily.

Originally, trading across international lines was tougher, with several different currencies involved across Europe. Though the main players within the European market were deeply involved in and veterans of international trade by the time other markets joined in, there have been more currencies to stay track of – the franc, the pound, the lira, and plenty of more – than was reasonable. With the birth of the eu Union in 1992, the wheels were set in motion to make one currency that will be used across most of Europe, and therefore the Euro was finally established and put into circulation in 1999.

Forex Today

While some countries have still not accepted the currency as their own (such as Britain, who still uses the sterling pound), the method of currency conversion has been simplified without the big number of assorted currencies that were previously controlled. Rather than dozens of currencies, the most countries interchange five – U.S. dollars, Australian dollars, British pounds sterling, the Euro, and also the Japanese Yen.

Today, the interchange Market is international and worldwide. The market is open 24 hours on a daily basis, 5 days per week, to accommodate all of the time zones for all of the most important players. These now include most of Europe, the u.s, and Asian markets, especially Japan. Even

Australia has joined the international trading markets, and since such nations are halfway round the world from a number of the opposite top players, time zones obviously must be taken into consideration.

Another completely separate but perhaps more important concern with trading in Forex is knowing how trade works in multiple currencies. How are you able to compare the worth of a stock across international lines if the values are expressed in two separate, non-equivalent currencies? And the way does one measure gains and losses when conversion rate is consistently changing?

Chapter 4: Understanding Currency Conversion

When you begin trading on Forex, you have got to find out the way to convert currencies and note the difference in values, also as how currencies are exchanged between international lines. This implies studying not only domestic market trends and currency values, but also those of foreign markets.

Working with Multiple Currencies

Since Forex is that the exchange Market, you obviously cannot expect everyone within the market to exchange U.S. dollars (and why not, you would possibly ask? – but remember that not everyone covets the U.S. dollar). With such a large amount of variables and volatile currencies being exchanged, how are you able to know an honest buy or sell once you see one without complete awareness of the worth of foreign currency?

The first step is to seek out a source that may provide you with a basic idea of this rate of exchange between your domestic currency and also the foreign currency in question. You ought to try this as a base listing for any currency that with which you would possibly get entangled. Of course, this cannot be consistent all the way down to the cent or fraction of a selected currency throughout a complete business day, but a minimum of you may have your to start} from which to begin, almost like North on a compass. Such sources will be found everywhere the web, furthermore as through many brokers, both on line and head to head.

Currency Expression

It is also good to grasp the means by which the currency conversion is expressed. The comparison is sometimes made in a very ratio called the cross-rate. During this configuration, the 2 currencies are listed in an XXX/YYY ratio, with the XXX position stated because the base currency. The bottom currency is sometimes expressed as a full number, while the YYY position is expressed because the decimal that almost all closely matches the based currency rate. It's kind of like making relevancy miles per gallon or rotations per minute on a car – a right away comparison of 1 to the opposite within the kind of a ratio.

The smallest fraction, or decimal, within which a currency may be traded, is termed a pip and this can be usually the degree to which a cross-rate is expressed. For instance, if country British pound may be traded in thousandths, the currency are expressed to the third decimal place. The U.S. dollar is usually expressed to the hundredth of a cent (the fourth decimal place).

In one cross-rate expression example, one U.S. dollar is also adore 117.456 Japanese yen. This ratio would be expressed as 1.000/117.456. The bottom currency is nearly always expressed as one unit (as in one dollar as critical ten dollars), and often that unit of measurement is that the U.S. dollar. Since the full number value (or big figure, because it is referred to) of the secondary currency, or the currency within the YYY position in terms of conversion changes so infrequently, often only the decimal portion of the quantity is mentioned within the exchange Market.

Therefore, within the ratio above, you'll hear that the yen is trading at .456, with no mention in any respect of the 117 whole yen that's shown within the ratio. This is often because the rate may vary from 117.456 to 117.423, but to not 119.024. Experiencing a change within the big figure – the entire number prior to the decimal – unless it had been only because the quantity was already within some thousandths, would represent much overlarge a shift in value for one trading period and would be a rare occurrence that would cause the complete market to create a drastic swing in one direction or the opposite.

The most common currencies found in Forex are the U.S. dollar, British people British monetary unit, the Euro, the Japanese yen, and also the dollar. Within the past, there would are more currencies to stay track of (such because the franc, the lira, or the Deutschmark). However, with the consolidation of most of the ecu market trading on Forex to the Euro, many currencies are eliminated, making trade on Forex for other lands easier.

If you get a commodity in an exceedingly particular currency, which currency's value falls against the U.S. dollar, you'll be able to actually make money by selling that very same commodity in dollars. The identical is true in reverse should the worth of a far off currency increase against a U.S. dollar. Of course, you'll be able to only cash in of such a situation should the commodity be traded in both currencies and both markets in question. We'll discuss this process, also as other ways to require advantage of the exchange Market (like arbitrage) in additional depth in future chapters.

Once you're able to discern a base value of every particular currency and its conversion rate against others traded on Forex, you may be ready to more closely monitor the change in currency conversion, including its inconsistency and volatility. Such ideas won't seem so "foreign", and you may be held and knowledgeable all along with the pros. Then, you may have to learn the way to read, understand, and ultimately interpret additional market trends.

Forex Trending

Following charts, paying attention to the recommendation of market analysts and chartists, and learning to create educated predictions yourself will facilitate your keep track of varied marketing trends. The following chapter will explain more about using the statistics that are published to forecast the following progress the exchange. Will it's a transparent, calm day with little activity, or is there a storm brewing with winds of change and uncertainty? How are you able to tell what's going to happen together with your holdings the subsequent day or perhaps further into the future?

Simply learning to read market trends can remove plenty of natural apprehension and uncertainty for beginning traders. In fact, sometimes the simplest opening to entering the market is to look at shows about it or read the financial sections of the newspaper that detail the trends and expected outcomes. The subsequent chapter will explain more about a way to interpret the statistics and basic trends.

Chapter 5: Understanding Statistics

You have now become somewhat accustomed to how the securities market works, and you understand to some extent what's involved in trading on the interchange Market. Now, you'd wish to understand how to measure market trends so as to make the most of your business ventures on the open market. We aren't any longer discussing penny stocks and playground games. You would like the real goods.

The name of the sport is statistics, and therefore the first rule is that you just must bear in mind there's no such thing as a certainty on the exchange. While you'll be able to never be 100% sure at any given time of the following move which will be made on the market as an entire, having the ability to read statistics and interpret them will place you sooner than the pack with reference to "guessing" what is going to happen next.

Investing could be a lot like gambling. If you'll keep track of the cards that have already been played, you're more informed, statistically, regarding what's likely to be dealt next, meaning you'll be able to place a bet with greater insight than someone who has no clue what has already been played. With the open market, if you have got information on what has already occurred over the past few days, months, or maybe years, you're again placed in a very better position to more logically conclude what is going to happen next. You merely learn the pattern and follow it to the top, reaping the financial rewards.

Charts and Chartists

Wait, did you think that you were visiting must research and map the market's past all by yourself? In fact not! There are people that get paid to try and do that kind of labor. They monitor the market hourly, daily, weekly, monthly, and yearly in order that they will provide big-time traders with the identical knowledge mentioned before. The more an investment firm knows about the market, the more cash they'll make. The identical is true for stockbrokers. They create money once you make money, and that they want to try to the most effective they'll to form sure that you just make intelligent decisions.

The best a part of this can be that you just have access to the identical information as these VIP clients. Chartists, who are essentially market analysts that publish their findings in easy to read charts, produce what's brought up as a candlestick chart. These charts are basically a mixture of a line graph and a bar chart that show the trend of varied stocks, indexes, or other interests over a specified period of your time. Therefore, you'll be able to easily determine if the commodity is on an uptrend or if it's taking a downturn, when the last major change occurred, and the way long it's predicted that the stock or bond will continue on this path.

You can actually find information on most commodities and their market trends for years within the past, and a few even all the way back to their introduction to the open market. Using this information can facilitate your decide whether it's an honest idea to shop for or sell the stocks or securities during which you have got interest, or if it's better to carry off for a peak within the market trend.

Understanding Market Trends

Understandably, as economies vary, the worth of varied commodities can change. This is often because, when an economy is powerful and flourishing, a nation is wealthier and has more purchasing power. Together with that power comes a better value for the things purchased. In other words, if people have extra money to spend and are spending a greater amount of that cash at Walmart stores, the worth of stock at Walmart goes to multiply at a substantial rate. Therefore, stockholders become wealthier in terms of assets, just because the consumers are driving the market with their purchasing power. When stockholders are wealthy, and therefore the value of their holdings is on the increase, they still purchase stock, which again, pumps the economy. A powerful upward trend within the exchange is a superb sign for any economy.

However, there are things that affect the market in a very negative fashion, causing stock values to plummet. As an example, warfare rarely encompasses a positive effect on the exchange. On terrorist attack, 2001, when terrorists attacked the globe Trade Center in NY City, the economy of the US took a large dive, and also the nation was threatened with a depression. Some analysts were sure that it might never properly recover. The identical thing typically happens any time there's an attack or act of war within a nation. However, the critics proved to be wrong, and also the u.s.

proceeded to rebound, or endure a foul downtrend, during a strong manner. This quick recovery occurred mostly because the people of the U. S. continued to push and spend, forcing money and wealth back to the economy. In watching the reaction of the stock exchange, you'll be able to learn to read trends supported world events.

Oil prices commonly affect the stock exchange, as well. Especially on the interchange Market, you'll find trends vary betting on many current events. You'll also note that, over time, the principle value (or face value) of a currency may purposely be revised by a nation in terms of currency conversion. This is often stated as devaluation, which can be discussed in greater detail within the following chapter.

Chapter 6: Forex Volatility and Market Expectation

Volatility, or the tendency for fluctuation that may affect your earnings within the exchange, is typical within a domestic market but even more evident and far stronger on the interchange Market. What factors affect the worth of currency on Forex, and is there any thanks to control this?

Devaluation and Revaluation

As mentioned within the previous chapter, devaluation refers to the purposeful decline in value of a currency in relevance other currencies as charged by a government entity. as an example, if the U. S. dollar is worth ten units of an overseas currency that's then devalued by one-tenth, the U. S. dollar is now corresponding to only nine units of the foreign currency. This makes any items purchased within the foreign currency costlier for those trading in U. S. dollars, because the charge per unit is lowered. It also makes items within the foreign country more cost-effective to interchange U. S. dollars.

An opposite change in value may occur, raising the worth of the foreign currency. This is often observed as revaluation. While it's going to seem that purposely adjusting the worth of a nation's currency is "cheating", or taking an unfair advantage by making foreign products cheaper to buy and increasing the worth of exports, there are regulations in situ to stop the manipulation of exchange rates for such purposes. The charter of the IMF (International Monetary Fund) assists in prohibiting such occurrences and enforcing the policy.

There are ways during which you'll profit of devaluation and revaluation, which is able to be discussed anon. However, what happens when the worth of a far off currency changes thanks to market fluctuation instead of purposeful reductions or increases by a central or federal bank? What effect do appreciation and depreciation wear the securities market?

Appreciation and Depreciation

Depreciation will be easily associated with the lifetime of a car. As soon as you drive a brand new car off the lot, the worth is sort of cut in half. This can be extreme depreciation. However, over the subsequent few years, the car continues to lose value at a more gradual pace. This can be considered to be depreciation yet.

Currency appreciation and depreciation are changes within the value of the currency that are driven by economic process instead of by government mandate. For instance, in an endeavor to repay certain loans, in 1998 the financial organization of Russia announced the approaching devaluation of the ruble. The rate, which was currently six rubles per U.S. dollar, would over a period of your time change to 9.5 rubles per dollar, effectively a depreciation of 34%.

However, before the change, there was a widespread panic within the previous Communist nation, and therefore the value of the ruble dropped thanks to many of us in Russia opting to interchange their securities before maturity. During a single day, following the announcement, the Russian ruble was depreciated by a tremendous 25%.

The same variety of crisis occurred within the 1920's with the crash of the U.S. stock market. In this time, a nationwide panic set in, and other people rushed to the banks to withdraw cash that wasn't available or to interchange securities and stock options that weren't matured. In running to the bank, people actually caused the crash instead of escaped it.

On the flip side of the coin, too fast of an appreciation sets up a rustic for inflation, or a rise within the retail value of products sold to the general public supported currency valuation. While inflation is guaranteed to occur, it will be minimally tempered through the employment of the currency valuation.

Appreciation will be associated with a vehicle in addition. Often, men enjoy taking old cars and restoring them to their original beauty. In doing so; they drastically increase the worth of the vehicle or appreciate it.

The ever changing rates of currency conversion and volatility of the market create an inherent market risk, or every day to day potential to experience loss because of fluctuation in securities prices. There's no thanks to diversify this sort of risk, because it is usually visiting affect investment to a particular degree. However, some risk is offset by particular sorts of investments or ways of investing that are safer or protected.

We will take a glance at long and short positions, short sale, stop orders, and other ways to shield your investments from drastic loss in additional chapters. These options include the flexibility to preset your purchase or sell price for a selected commodity, similarly as using various predetermine order levels to put orders and complete transactions.

Of course, don't delude yourself into thinking that you simply can rid yourself of all possible risk factors on the market. There's always a cloud hanging over your head waiting to burst, and everyone it takes is one little pinprick. You want to always exercise caution, though the concept of playing the securities market entails danger and excitement inherently. the following chapter will facilitate your get a grasp on reality and what's involved in balancing your risk factor with a grounding in reality; your ego together with your id.

Chapter 7: Aspects of the Trade

You are now versed within the functionality of the exchange and have decided that you just are willing to simply accept the danger factors involved. However, you wish to grasp everything you'll be able to about balancing that risk with intelligent investment options. How are you able to make certain that the risks you're taking are more likely to be rewarding within the long term than destructive?

Long and Short

One of the foremost important parts of creating money on the securities market is to work out your position. The long position is largely the purchasing position – you're getting ready to tackle a long-term commitment for ownership of some stock, security, or other traded commodity. The short position, against this, is that the selling position – you're shortly visiting eliminate the identical kind of ownership and any responsibility toward it.

The best time to require up the long position is when stock prices are low. This can get you into the market at an inexpensive price and increase your chances for profitability as new offerings go up in price and older investment options recover or rebound. In fact, as others take the long position and get at the identical time you are doing, this may actually drive the worth of securities up through the quality rule of supply and demand, causing the start of what may well be a market.

You may equate this with the tip of the month at a car dealership. The costs tend to drop on any cars left on the lot available, and therefore the dealer is more often willing to bargain because he or she wants less inventory on the lot. Likewise, when stock prices are low, some will panic and dump all of their holdings at these low prices, thinking that their shares will never recover the worth. This could only be of assistance to you.

When prices are high, it's likely time to show around and sell your shares to herald a profit, not losing anything on unrealized gain (profit that can't be counted in quick assets or cash because it's still invested during a volatile stock option). You must never sell for a price that's below your cost, as this brings negative equity and loss of funds. You must always sell for the best amount of profit that you simply feel is safe.

In other words, if you purchase a security at fifteen dollars per share, and it quickly rises to 25 dollars per share, you will okay feel that it could hit thirty dollars per share within per week. However, you need to determine if you're willing to risk losing your already secured earnings of ten dollars per share to attend that long, should the value actually fall, so you will arrange to sell at the present high price.

Market-Makers and Selling Short

What if the stock values are up incredibly high, but you probably did not get in on it particular commodity and own no shares? Your start should be to go to a market-maker or to form a cope with a broker for a brief sell. A market-maker is literally a stockbroker who purchases keeps a particular amount of shares of several securities or stocks there, which are purchased during a time when the market rates are low.

The firm will then rotate and sell those shares to a private at that low price, no matter the market rate, in effect making its own market (thus the name). The individual who purchases from the firm can immediately sell the commodities on the open market at market rate (which is higher), making an implausible amount of profit during a short period of your time.

A short sell is another choice for a fast profit. During this scenario, you may borrow a selected number of shares from a stockbroker to sell when the market price is high. Your job is to then await the stock price to travel down, purchase the identical quantity of stock, and return the holdings to the broker, keeping the take advantage of the sale, minus the broker fees.

The way that a dealer works with trade-ins is extremely similar. They'll purchase the car from you at a really low price, then rotate and sell it on the lot for a high margin of profit.

One of the foremost positive aspects of a brief sell is that you simply never actually take possession of the stock, meaning that you just are never during a position to lose money. Because you have got sold shares for a high price, you've got already profited, and within the worst-case scenario, the actual stocks won't call in price. Instead of return the stocks to the broker from whom they were borrowed, you'll be able to simply pay back the number that they were originally purchased, together with the premium.

How are you able to make sure that you simply won't overshoot the most effective price options or miss an honest rate because you're unavailable to position a buy order or sell order along with your broker? Is there the way to line limits on your trades? Next, we'll discuss ways to guard your investments and limit your risk factors.

Chapter 8: Risk Management

One of the foremost important aspects of protecting your investments is balancing your risks with reassurances. There are several ways to try and do this, and that we will discuss those during this chapter.

Limit Orders and Balancing Risks

A limit order may be a standing amount at which you've got agreed to shop for or sell a selected security or other commodity. As an example, you have got designated to your stockbroker that you simply won't sell X Security until its value reaches a minimum value of Y dollars. At the identical time, you'll not purchase the identical X Security if it exceeds a worth of Z. Setting limits for the worth you pay money for a specific security, similarly because the price you'll accept to sell it, protects you and your investment in several ways.

First of all, you're maximizing your gains, but mostly, you're avoiding loss. Any loss that happens with limit orders will always be unrealized loss, or a loss that's not measurable in quick assets or cash. In other words, until you sell the stock and reap the online loss, it'll not affect your net worth. Since you have got set a limit that doesn't allow your commodities to be sold for fewer than the initial cost, you can't possibly have a loss in your net worth. At the identical time, you're also assuring a minimum of a particular amount of profit by setting your sell point high enough to reap that specific profit.

Another way to safeguard your assets is to hedge. This implies that you simply create and sell a derivative instrument stating that, when your shares reach a specific value within the future, you'll sell your holdings at this predetermined price. When that price is reached, the order are going to be processed and therefore the transaction completed. Of course, if you ever change your mind a few limit that you simply have set, you'll place an order along with your broker, which designates that you simply not wish to trade at the desired dollar amount.

You can also buy on margin. This is often very kind of like trading, but rather than borrowing stocks to sell, you're essentially borrowing money to buy stocks on your own when the value is down. Then, when the worth of the securities you have got purchased rises and you're ready to sell for a profit, you repay the loan and keep the surplus from the sell, minus the broker fees. Of course, all dealings with a stockbroker incur a premium, or fee for services rendered, and it's nearly impossible to trade without a broker or broker service. However, online services are often less costly than live agents, but you'll research to work out what your best choice is.

How Do I Handle a Whipsaw?

No, we don't seem to be pertaining to anything within the garage, the bedroom, or a rustic band. A whipsaw is market trend that defies the percentages. It will be thought of because the "fender bender". Despite how careful you're as you learn to drive a car and become coordinated, sometimes you can't do anything to avoid being rear-ended.

Whipsaw could be a term for what happens when everything points toward a selected direction in market trend, causing you to shop for (if it's like prices are visiting rise) or sell (if it seems they're on the brink of fall), then the other effect occurs.

For example, if you buy a security at five dollars per share because the stock seems to possess fallen as far because it can go and appears to be starting an upward trend, then unexpectedly, the stock plummets to at least one dollar per share, this can be considered a whipsaw effect. If this happens to you, because it surely will if you play the market long enough, the simplest thing to try and do is wait it out. The stock will do one amongst two things – it'll either dissolve entirely, and also the company will go bankrupt (this is what you are doing not want to happen), or it'll rebound, and you'll be able to value more highly to look forward to an opportunity to show a profit otherwise you can get out as soon because the purchase rate is reached.

Whipsaws don't seem to be the top of the globe, and nobody can expect to realize with every stock exchange purchase. However, if you discover that you just are involved in several of those instances, you must seriously reconsider your investment options. You will be reading the signs incorrectly, otherwise you can be picking bad stocks. You must seek advice for any future investments you expect to create before purchasing any longer stocks or securities.

Another way to overturn a foul investment like this is often to proceed with an offset transaction – an acquisition or sell that offsets the loss of a previous transaction. you may either purchase additional stock within the same company at the lower cost if you expect it to recover, otherwise you can go for another hot commodity that's close to explode in price, either of which can facilitate your offset your loss. you may also sell shares of a security within which you have got an outsized amount of unrealized gain – gain that can't be measured in quick assets or cash thanks to increase in value of stock and security holdings – so as to exchange the lost cash value.

All of those are viable options to recover a loss, but looking ahead to the share value to rebound is usually the primary choice. It avoids the loss of funds already invested, retains the choice to pursue profit, and reduces the chance of further investment into the market.

As you grow and study these various options, you may have to feel more leisurely when surrounded by financial gurus and geeks who speak what looks like gibberish, muttering words you've got never heard left and right. The subsequent chapter will take you thru a number of the meanings of the main "buzz" words employed in the securities market and therefore the international financial district.

Chapter 9: Buzz Words

Now that you just know a touch more about the securities market, and you've got decided to do your hand at investment, you ought to be more concerned with understanding the jargon you'll hear on the trading room floor. Although you most likely won't end up amid a bunch of screaming stockbrokers on Wall Street (and nowadays, most of the trading is finished by computer anyway), knowing that learning to speak the talk is a component of walking the walk.

Margins, Spreads, and Other Condiments

Okay, so it's margins, not margarines, but it sounds very similar. So as to know the stock exchange, especially on Forex, you would like to talk not a language meant for common communication, but the language of trade. For example, once you think about a margin, for several this suggests a variable – just like the "margin of error" in a very statistic.

However, in trade, it refers to the sum of cash borrowed from a broker so as to buy stocks when the market is on a downtrend. Then, when the worth begins its next upswing, you sell the stock at the upper price, pay back the margin (along with the premium accrued), and retain the profit.

When you buy on margin, the cash lent by the stockbroker is mentioned as a brokerage account. The brokerage account is provisional supported the worth of the stock. Occasionally, if the worth of the stocks purchased should drop too low for the security margin set forth by the broker, the agent will request that extra money be deposited into the brokerage account to create up for loss. This can be cited as a call.

In some trades, the market price doesn't get play. As an example, a forward trade is about up between two individuals or two companies outside the open market. It involves a process of negotiation and an eventual compromise in price. There's usually a bid made – the offer to shop for a commodity at a specific price – and a price or offer – the worth that the opposite business entity is willing to sell the securities or other holdings. The difference between these two purchase numbers is observed because the spread.

If the spread can't be narrowed and eventually closed, no deal will be made. This agreed-upon price is named the forward price, and every one details involved within the trade process when this sort of transaction takes place are detailed in a very contract and noted as forward points. Usually, the forward price is made public as available for a specific date, and will the transaction not be completed on this date (referred to because the transaction date), then the trade must be renegotiated.

Jobbers, Yards, and Other "Brit" Terms

One of the most important foreign markets that Americans trading on Forex will encounter is that of British. While several other terms referring to the securities market are similar thanks to the common language, there are some specific terms that are very different within the British trading vocabulary.

For example, within the u. s., stockbrokers who hold onto securities purchased at low prices for the aim of selling them to clients in a very higher priced market (so that the client can rotate and resell them for the profit on the open market) are called market-makers. However, in Britain, this sort of investor is just cited as a "jobber".

Another term you'll want to be conversant in is "yard". This doesn't check with a green patch of land, a measurement in inches, or perhaps 36 of something. The term is employed in relevance quantity of currency instead of value and is admire 1,000,000 units of the currency in question. In other words, you'll be able to have a yard of dollars or a yard of yen, and though it's the identical quantity of bills, coins, or whatever physical currency is employed, it's not necessarily equivalent in value.

In Britain, they are doing not use the Euro, and that they don't use the U.S. dollar. They need chosen to still use the quid, a currency that has been employed in the country for many years. However, Britain is currently on a path to create the conversion to the Euro within the subsequent five years.

Open and Shut

In the exchange, there are various sorts of orders that may be placed to assist protect you from making a nasty investment or to limit the quantity you buy a specific security or other commodity. As an example, if you have got made a foul investment and don't want to reinvest in a very particular security, you ought to sell all shares of that stock, irrespective of absorbing tiny low loss. This action is mentioned as closing an edge. On the contrary, if you're doing well along with your investment, you may participate in a very rollover, simply reinvesting any earnings in additional shares of the stock or security.

An military formation is strictly what it feels like, meaning that the order remains pending until it's either executed by your stockbroker or canceled by you because the client. A stop-loss order would cancel any pending orders you've got placed together with your stockbroker. You furthermore may have options like One Cancels the opposite Orders. These allow you to own interest in several commodities, leaving orders together with your stockbroker to shop for all of them, should they drop to a specific price. Then, should one among those reach this preset low price, your stockbroker will follow your direction and invest your money in this particular security, followed by a cancellation of all additional orders.

When a broker gives you an estimate on the value for a selected stock or commodity, it's considered a quote. A quote isn't completely accurate and is typically noted as a damage, because the value of a security can change within some seconds. However, it's as near accurate as are often expected. After you put in an order, the broker then processes the fill, or completion, of that order. The particular value at which the trade is completed is named the fill price. The completion of a trade or purchase, brought up as a settlement, may be called the execution of a transaction or realization of an order. As you see, there are plenty of terms to require into consideration, and that we haven't even begun to think about terms utilized in a number of the tougher areas of the market.

Next, we'll consider some specialized, more complex trading options that you just can use on Forex to require advantage of the volatility of the market and also the constantly varying exchange rates.

Chapter 10: Expert Trading Options

After spending lots of your time buying and trading on both domestic and foreign markets, you may find that the method becomes easier and almost intuitive. You not should work so hard to work out currency conversion or find the following big explosive commodity. It'll be like wont for you.

What, then, becomes the following big challenge for somebody trading on the open market? What keeps things from becoming monotonous and boring? First of all, there's always something new and different happening on the exchange Market. Remember, it operates 24 hours on a daily basis, and you never know what you may find once you get up within the morning. However, there are various ways in which you'll profit of the variance in currency conversion and a lag in time between markets that may affect trading values.

Arbitrage

There are some commodities that are traded in multiple currencies on multiple markets on Forex. Although computers have made worldwide communication almost lightning fast nowadays, all of those markets can trade along with fairly equivalent values for the securities shared across currencies.

However, the system isn't perfect, and also the value may rise or fall in one country and currency before the identical change in value reaching across another border. Seasoned traders have learned to require advantage of this lag within the market trending by employing a process called arbitrage. During this transaction, you get the actual stock or security on the market with the cheaper price while simultaneously selling the identical in a very market where the worth is higher. The method may be a bit complex, so we'll use an example. Let's say that one U.S. dollar is appreciate .5 British pounds, meaning that everything goes to be twice as expensive in British pounds.

Now, let's take a glance at the value of a stock that's traded on both markets. If they were equivalent, then the stock would trade for 2 dollars within the U.S. and one pound in Britain. However, if something happens and therefore the stock value drops in Britain, it's six hours prior to the u. s., and this drop might not hit the American market immediately.

If the worth of the stock drops in Britain to .8 pounds, the acquisition price is now below that of the value in dollars because of the currency conversion. During this case, arbitrage would occur once you bought shares of the stock in on a people market in pounds and sold it on the U.S. market in dollars, benefiting by the slow communication of the autumn in value of the stock. In effect, you'll make $.40 per stock.

Volatility of Currency Conversion

Another way to require advantage of the ever-shifting value of every individual currency is to trade supported the changing rates. What exactly does this involve? You need to closely watch the changing conversion rates. When a currency conversion rate changes drastically, it's time to create a move. this is often very the same as arbitrage, but the realm is far riskier thanks to high volatility. for example, if you have got purchased a stock within the scenario above on the U.S. marketplace for two dollars a share, and suddenly nation pound gains value, dropping to a conversion of only half a pound for each two dollars, you'd want to sell your shares on a people market because the worth of a pound is higher and now has greater purchasing power.

One piece of recommendation to stay in mind, though, is that it's best to instantly lose all assets in foreign currency, usually within the same day. this is often named as tomorrow next because it takes two to 3 business days for foreign currency to be delivered, and by exchanging the currency for value in stocks on the identical business day, you avoid having to require delivery of the currency altogether.

Chapter 11: Other Trading Options

Besides the expert options described above, there are other nontraditional ways to form money on the stock exchange. In considering these options, however, you must consider making a career of trading stocks and securities. Some kinds of trading are simply not for the faint of heart, which means you need to have complete motivation and an adventurous spirit to require part in these areas of the market. the probabilities of taking an enormous hit and experiencing an excellent loss are multiplied.

Day Trading

Day traders tackle a number of the best market risk of all. Because day traders work with investments that change drastically within hours, they're naturally playing within the lion's den. These stocks are extremely volatile, and for many, day trading could be a quick thanks to lose a good deal of cash. it's difficult to create a good deal of money during this manner, and it's even harder to forecast the end result of those day trade stock options. you can't make certain of the overnight position (the net value at which a stockbroker or day trader will open the subsequent morning).

And in Forex, there's little room for day trading, because the market never shuts down during the workweek. In these cases, the day trader should set a limit for him- or herself to urge out, selling all shares, in order that he or she will sleep soundly while the planet spins round and begin the subsequent day fresh.

Day trading is incredibly dangerous and isn't recommended to newcomers. In fact, it's not really recommended in the least, and the general public who partake of this volatile a part of the industry are extremely seasoned in trading on the open market, don't consider the danger factors carefully enough before entering this branch of the market, or have enough money that they simply wish to do this type of investment and don't care if they lose a goodly sum.

Secondary Markets

Secondary markets are interesting therein they're created by the govt. to assist redistribute money that's used for loans. corporation and Freddie Mac are two of the most important corporations from which stocks are purchased on a secondary market.

Here is how it works. When an individual purchases a home, he or she requests a loan from the bank, usually for about eighty percent of the value of the house. this can be granted, and therefore the home is purchased by the bank for the individual or family, who begins to pay off the loan to the bank.

Meanwhile, to assure that cash is on the market at that bank for the subsequent one that needs a real estate loan, Fannie Mae or Federal Home Loan Mortgage Corporation, two entities originally established by the us government, will purchase the loan from the bank. Therefore, the money is returned to the bank to be used within the future.

What do these agencies then do with the deficit they need acquired? They sell it. On the secondary market, they slash the loan into shares that are backed by the mortgage itself and sell those shares, recovering the cash from investors. Eventually, those securities mature, probably about the identical time that the initial loan is paid off to the bank, and also the investors reap the advantages of their investment with the interest earned.

Another way to require advantage of a volatile international stock exchange is to create a swap. this is often the exchange of securities or bonds so as to require advantage of lower interest rates. as an example, if a business entity in Britain is in possession of 1 security, and another in Japan is in possession of a special security, the 2 commodities could also be beneficially traded or sold to every other so as to save lots of on the interest rates, if the currently held bond or security is kept at a lower charge per unit within the opposing market.

For example, let's say one business is in possession of a bond "A" that's paying out only two percent interest in its current market, and another is holding bonds "B" in its market at three percent interest. If bond A is truly paying out three percent on the foreign market, and bond B may be cashed certain four percent on the primary market, both parties can make more cash on a trade of bonds. they'll mutually have the benefit of a purchase of the securities to every other because of a gain of more interest.

If that seems confusing, then perhaps a swap isn't in your near future. This is often more often processed between businesses on the foreign market instead of individual parties, though with the proper broker, it may well be accomplished. However, do you have to work the deal, you would like know little except that you just are viewing a better ratio than previously, and your broker will make sure of the remainder.

If you identify that you simply should have stock options as a business, you'll probably arrange to hire a fulltime consultant for all of your financial needs, including the handling of your share holdings. In fact, when businesses are large enough and present a powerful enough trading presence within the market, especially on Forex, you may find that there are entire departments dedicated to maintenance on the stock options.

Chapter 12: In Review

After shoveling through piles of knowledge and taking in most knowledge, you most likely want you're swimming in terminology and can't remember just where to start. the most effective thanks to retain knowledge is thru repetition, and having a fast reference guide is rarely a nasty idea, either. the subsequent pages are a short overview of the thorough discussions during this book, allowing you to quickly reference a subject in an exceedingly bind.

The Basic Trade

A share may be a holding of an organization that varies in value supported the will or need for that specific company's goods or services. As a shareholder, your net worth increases and reduces supported taking a brief position (selling) when values are high and an extended position (buying) when prices are low. As long because the stock or security is in your possession, the change in value is taken into account unrealized gain or loss because you can't measure it in quick assets (cash).

When most commodities traded on the market are on a robust upward trend for a period of your time, this can be cited as a market. Should value take a pointy downward swing and continue thereon path, it's called a market. If no such trend is recognized, and therefore the value of stocks and securities is fairly even, this is often said as flat.

The exchange Market

The interchange Market is that the stock market on which several different countries across several different time zones trade their domestic and international commodities in various currencies. Currency is that the denomination or monetary division utilized in a specific land (such because the U.S. dollar or the Euro). When multiple currencies are in use, they're typically expressed as a ratio called a cross-rate that shows the number of a second currency that's akin to the primary listed. Determining what the equivalent is would be mentioned as currency conversion.

Several countries in Europe, which have now consolidated their currencies to agree on the Euro (since 1999) trade on Forex, because it is named for brief. Britain, which to the current point has opted to continue using the British pound, also takes part in international trade, similarly because the us, Japan, and Australia. Each of those countries utilizes its own currency for normal trading purposes, with options for investment in foreign currencies. Determining whether or not this is often worthwhile depends on the currency conversion rate.

The value of a nation's currency is decided by its government and federal bank (the central bank, better referred to as the FED, is that the federal bank of the United States). Purposeful change within the rate of conversion by a government is noted as valuation – devaluation is taking value and strength from the currency, and revaluation adds strength and get power to the currency. If the identical change to the speed of conversion occurs naturally through events and therefore the volatility of the market, it's then called appreciation and depreciation.

Careers within the Market

Without the help of execs, it's nearly impossible to trade on the open market. Market analysts track trends within the stock exchange that affect the worth of share holdings. They use such information and basic history to assist predict the result of various aspects of the market within the future.

Other individuals, cited as chartists, create charts and graphs that interpret all the info – various numbers, statistics, percentages, etc – into a simple to read candlestick chart that tracks the trends of specific commodities on the market.

A stockbroker is a private or a corporation that assists you in making your investments. A broker can aid you in making smart financial decisions, helping you track your and place your orders, and following trends within the market.

A market-maker does the identical job as a stockbroker, with the exception that this individual or company retains an investment in an exceedingly particular type of securities and bonds which will be sold in brief order to a client for a lower cost so the client can make money by immediately selling the identical shares at the upper market value.

Other individuals can assist with loans, allowing you to shop for on margin. This involves the alternative approach – borrowing money to get a stock or security that's at an occasional market price in order that the client can later resell the commodity at the next price.

Protecting Your Investments

There are several ways to guard your investments. By placing limit orders, you guarantee to the simplest of your ability that you just won't lose money on the market and virtually guarantee a minimum of a minimal profit. However, if you modify your mind about those limits, you'll always place a stop-loss order. If you permit standing instructions together with your stockbroker, these are spoken as open orders that remain such until the transaction is executed and therefore the order filled.

Try to set your limit orders just above the support levels (the lowest levels of import to which a stock can drop) and just under the amount of resistance (the upper level above which it's difficult for the worth of a stock to rise).

Also, set a price date – a date at which era you'll take a median of the worth of a selected commodity and review your options. this could be reviewed a minimum of every six months, if you intend to retain any holdings of a specific security.

Chapter 13: One Final Option

While "Chapter 13" isn't an appropriate thanks to end a financial endeavor, it is, during this case, one in all the foremost important conclusions to an incredibly helpful tool filled with investment advice, especially when it's placed at the top of a book to supply assistance to those threatened with bankruptcy because of bad investment decisions. There are always ways to show around after you have begun to steer down the incorrect path. very like moving on to a replacement car after purchasing a lemon that has been nothing but a nightmare, you'll be able to reverse your direction.

Some people can spend days, months, and even years trying to overcome the stock exchange and still fail. In some cases, it's virtually impossible for a personal to ever get the hang of the functionality of the market. If you can not follow market trends, then it's best that you simply don't make any investment decisions.

It is okay to not fit into the market. At the identical time, you'll be able to still make money with investments. One final option you have got is to form a discretionary account. this suggests that you just sign a contract together with your stockbroker and switch over a sum of cash to the agent for investment, leaving the determination of placement of that investment within the hands of your agent. You nevermore should worry that you simply have made a nasty investment. In fact, during this scenario, you are doing not even should follow any market trends or other information that has anything to try and do with financial investment. Your broker will simply allow you to know after you have increased your net worth or if your assets have taken a dive.

Whatever choices you create with regard to taking possession on the stock exchange, you would like not worry about not having the essential information to assist you get through your first few trading experiences. Now, you've got the essential knowledge and also the essential reference guide to induce you started on the trail to success and wealth that you simply can access at any given time.

www.ingramcontent.com/pod-product-compliance
Lightning Source LLC
Chambersburg PA
CBHW051538240526
45465CB00027B/707